Table of Contents

Preamble 6
Introduction 7
Fundamental Analysis 8
Technical Analysis 17
   Security Analysis 20
Conclusion 23

Preamble

This book presents a detailed case study in which McDonald's company is assessed and its stocks are analyzed to determine whether or not to invest in them. It is included in my book **Play Smart in the Stock Market – The 4 Keys to Success**, on sale at Amazon, where all concepts and techniques to assess the state of the stock market and invest in successful stocks with moderated risk are detailed. That is, to perform on your own the type of analyses presented hereunder. Of course, I strongly recommend you to read it.

All data used in this analysis are of financial closure 2013 except for the price of the shares, for which I took the most recent one (November 2014). Price charts shown are taken from http://finance.yahoo.com.

Finally, I want to make clear that this study is subjective and in no way attempts to convince the reader to buy or sell shares of McDonald's, but readers are encouraged to do their own research and make their own conclusions, just presented as an illustration of the methodology and the use of analysis tools that I discuss in my book **Play Smart in the Stock Market – The 4 Keys to Success**.

Introduction

McDonald's is the largest fast food restaurant chain in the world, serving 70 million customers each day at its 35,000 restaurants across 119 countries. Originally American and focused on the business of burgers and fries (although it recently expanded its offering with ice creams, salads, sandwiches, etc.), such is its international presence that The Economist has created the "McDonald's index," which compares the price of Big Macs (the flagship product of the company) in each country to provide a benchmark for the cost of living across countries, as well as for the value of local currencies against the USD.

McDonald's is listed in the New York Stock Exchange and belongs to the S&P-500 and Dow Jones indices, and its stocks closed 2013 at $97.03 (+10% in the year), yielding $3.12 dividends per share (3.21% per share), and has been paying dividends out for 38 consecutive years. Currently (November 2014), the stock is quoting at about $96, and there are 990 million shares outstanding, so the company capitalizes at $95,040 million.

We will analyze the company through the data published in its annual reports, including Form 10-K required by the U.S. Securities and Exchange Commission (SEC) of all listed companies and found in the following link:

http://www.aboutmcdonalds.com/content/dam/AboutMcDonalds/Investors/McDs2013AnnualReport.pdf

NOTE: all data used in this analysis are from the 2013 year-end (latest year report), except for the price of the shares for which the most recent was taken (November 2014).

Fundamental Analysis

McDonald's directly operates fully-owned and franchised restaurants from which it charges fees in concept of image rights, commercial, consulting, advertising, etc. Specifically, 67% of the company's global revenues (a total $28,106 million in 2013) are provided by owned restaurants. Franchisees contribute with the remaining 33%, even though 80% of the restaurants are franchises (profitability is much lower for franchisees but the risk is shared). Franchised revenues come from real estate rental, initial fees, and a percentage of sales.

Geographically, sales come from: the USA (31%), Europe (40%), APMEA (Asia-Pacific, Middle East and Africa) (23%), and other areas account for the remainder (6%). The main markets in Europe are the UK, France, Russia, and Germany (representing 67% of European revenues). Japan, China, and Australia are the greatest contributors from the Asia/Pacific area (representing 54% of APMEA revenues). These seven markets along with the USA and Canada are called the "major markets" and contribute with 75% of revenues. The company's geographical, political, and currency diversification is therefore very good.

Competitors are companies like Burger King, Starbucks, Chipotle, Yum!, or Tim Hortons (recently taken over by Burger King). In general, they are comparatively small businesses in all terms (profit, number of restaurants, and capitalization). For example, Burger King, which is the most like McDonald's, has 13,000 restaurants worldwide and annual revenues of $1,100 million. However, the main competition is Yum!, a group that manages brands such as Pizza Hut, KFC, and Taco Bell, and has similar figures to McDonald's and a significant presence in Asia.

McDonald's has grown in economic terms, albeit moderately, despite the global crisis of recent years (2% annually in recent years, although in some cases, as in 2012, McDonald's net profit decreased), and in 2013, the total number of restaurants increased by 1000. McDonald's also maintains a policy to return to investors all free-cash-flow generated via dividends and share repurchases.

The 2013 balance sheet is summarized as follows (figures rounded and expressed in billions of US dollars, data extracted from the consolidated annual report):

ASSETS	OWNERS' EQUITY & LIABILITIES
Non-current Assets 31,5	Owners' Equity 16
	Non-current Liabilities 20,5
Current Assets 5	Current Liabilities 3,1

The positive working capital of $1.9M (current assets less current liabilities = 5-3.1) enables the company to meet its short-term liabilities. The current ratio CA/CL is 1.61 so the company will have no problems meeting payments in the short term, but the ratio is a little high and may indicate some insignificant waste. In addition, long-term debts are fully covered by fixed assets.

McDonald's Owners' Equity (always positive or the company would be in a technical bankruptcy) represents a high percentage of total liabilities (40%), indicating that the company is solvent and is slightly externally indebted (debt = 23.6/16 = 1.48). Moreover, long-term debt is much higher (6.6 times) than the short-term debt. 60% of assets are financed by outside money (leverage ratio = 23.6/39.6 = 0.596). The book value of the company is $16 billion (the book value of each share would be about $16.20).

Going further into detail, we can calculate the working capital requirements (WCR), which are relatively low and completely covered by the working capital:

WCR = Accounts receivable + Inventory − Accounts payable − Accrued expenses
= 1.3 + 0.12 − 0.22 = $1.2 billions

The consolidated P&L statement (rounded and summarized) is (expressed in billions of US dollars):

+	Revenues	28.11 (100%)
−	Cost of Sales	17.2*
=	Gross Profit	10.9 (38.8%)
−	Operating Expenses	2,14**
=	EBITDA	8.76 (31.1%)
−	Amortizations/others	0.038
−	Provisions	0
=	EBIT	8.73 (31%)

+/-	Financial interests	-0.52
=	EBT	8.2 (29.2%)
-	Taxes	2.62 (32%)
=	Net Income	5.59 (19.9%)

* costs directly associated with both owned and franchised restaurants

** sales, administration, and other costs

EBIT represents 31% of revenues, which apparently is a good figure although a bit low if compared with that of Burger King (45%). In any case, net profit is 20% of revenues for both companies. This indicates that Burger King is more efficient in their operations but McDonald's is better funded, which is a reasonable conclusion as McDonald's is a much larger company (its revenues are about 25 times higher).

However Yum!, a company approximately half the size, has an EBIT of 14% and a net profit of 8% in comparison to total revenues, figures that have been significantly reduced from 2012 indeed; in this case the comparison heavily favors McDonald's.

Expenses are not very broken down, but we can guess that McDonald's has very low overheads and most of the expenses concentrate in restaurants, or in operations, which is a very good sign.

Return on assets (ROA = 5.59/36.5 = 15.3%) indicates that investments are well allocated and profit in a reasonably short period of time (6 years). The equity of shareholders (ROE = 5.59/16 = 35%) provides a very high yield (profitability in 3 years).

Geographically, McDonald's EBIT (Operating Income) is higher in the USA and Europe (where there is higher concentration of owned restaurants) and has only declined in APMEA (-6%) when compared to 2012. The highest sales were achieved in Europe.

ZONE	REVENUES	EBIT	%EBIT	Var.
USA	4.512	3.779	83,7%	+1%
Europe	8.138	3.371	41,4%	+5%
APMEA	5.425	1.480	27,3%	-6%
Others	800	134	16,75%	+46%
TOTAL	28.106	8.764	31,2%	+2%

As for cash, the company had $2.8 billion (US billions, i.e. thousands of millions) at 2013 year end, which is 22% more than in 2012, and cash-flow is therefore positive. The operations contributed with $7.1 billion to the cash-flow throughout the year, of which $3 billion where paid out as dividends. With these data and the low financial interest, we can conclude that cash is not a problem for the company.

Some more interesting information can be obtained from the report:

- The company spent $1,810 billion in treasury stock (purchase of shares of the company from other shareholders).

- Annual growth objectives of the company are: revenues 3-5%, EBIT 6-7%, and ROIIC (return on investment) around 20%.
- The currency exchange had a negative impact on the company's accounts
- 1,400 new restaurants opened in 2013, while around 500 closed down.
- $2.8 billion was reinvested (CapEx), split approximately fifty-fifty between new and existing restaurants.
- 74% of debt is fixed rate so the risk is low, although 41% is in foreign currency so there is high exposure to currency fluctuations (particularly the euro).
- Average interest rate paid on the debt is 3% (0.065% for long-term debt and 5.1% for short-term debt).
- Operations generate as much cash as 50% of total debt.
- The company owns 658 million shares (treasury stock) against a total of 1.648 million (an additional 990 million are free-floating), meaning 40%, a relatively high figure that would reduce the possibility of speculation by large investors and hostile enterprises and would add stability to its stock price.

Let's value the company by means of the Discounted Cash-Flow (DCF) method. Although this method is somewhat subjective and complex, we can still perform simplified calculations to get an idea of the approximate value of the company based on its cash-making ability.

We will estimate future cash-flows for the next four years (2014, 2015, 2016, and 2017) from past free-cash-flow data (in so doing, we are assuming that the company will keep performing the same way). Thus, the net present value (NPV) of the company is calculated from these estimated cash-flows:

$$NPV = \frac{CF_{2014}}{(1+k)^1} + \frac{CF_{2015}}{(1+k)^2} + \frac{CF_{2016}}{(1+k)^3} + \frac{CF_{2017} + VR_{2017}}{(1+k)^4}$$

We could review past annual reports to extract free-cash-flow data for each year, but there is nothing more foolish than to re-work. Some professional websites have already done it for us, for example Ycharts.com (http://ycharts.com/companies/ MCD / free_cash_flow). Here are the FCF data from the past 8 years, according to Ychart:

Year	FCF ($ billions)	Var.
2013	$4,3	+10%
2012	$3,9	-11%
2011	$4,4	+5%
2010	$4,2	+10%
2009	$3,8	+0%
2008	$3,8	+31%
2007	$2,9	+11%
2006	$2,6	-

Average FCF for the last four years is $4.2 billion with an annual incremental trend of 8% since 2006. In addition, after the first two quarters of 2014, the FCF is foreseen to increase in 2014 (improvement at mid-2014 is 14%), which is a great sign. Therefore, we can assume future cash-flow to increase by 8% each year from the $4.2 billion average:

Year	Cash-Flow
2014	4,54
2015	4,89
2016	5,29
2017	5,71

We now have to calculate the discount rate (k) using the WACC formula, knowing that the company pays 3% on average for its debt and considering that investors demand an extra 16% annual profit (3% dividend rate plus 13% on capital gains due to the share price rise, which is the average of the last five years):

$$WACC = \frac{k_d D(1-t) + k_e E}{D+E} = \frac{0,03 * 23,6 * (1-0,32) + 0,16 * 16}{23,6 + 16} = 7,68\%$$

It is also necessary to calculate the residual value of the company at 2017, because we will never calculate the cash-flow from that year to infinity. Assuming a constant long-term growth rate (g) of 3% (this is another great estimate):

$$RV_{2017} = \frac{CF_{2017}(1+g)}{(k-g)} = \frac{5,71 * (1+0,03)}{(0,0768 - 0,03)} = \$125,76 \; billions$$

Finally, the value of the company is:

$$NPV = \frac{CF_{2014}}{(1+k)^1} + \frac{CF_{2015}}{(1+k)^2} + \frac{CF_{2016}}{(1+k)^3} + \frac{CF_{2017} + VR_{2017}}{(1+k)^4} =$$

$$= \frac{4{,}54}{(1+0{,}0768)^1} + \frac{4{,}89}{(1+0{,}0768)^2} + \frac{5{,}29}{(1+0{,}0768)^3} + \frac{5{,}71 + 125{,}76}{(1+0{,}0768)^4} = \$110{,}46 \; billions$$

Dividing this figure by the number of shares of the company (990 million free-floating), we obtain the theoretical value of the shares: **$111.57**.

You can compare this value with professional assessments such as that by Stock Analysis On Net (http://www.stock-analysis-on.net/NYSE/Company/McDonalds-Corp/DCF/Present-Value-of-FCFF#Intrinsic-Stock-Value), which estimates the value of McDonald's stock at $114.80 and is probably conducted by far more complex and difficult-to-understand calculations, as well as that of www.gurufocus.com, whose estimate is $108.56.

In conclusion, as the company stock now trades at around $96 (November 2014), we could state it is undervalued (with a safety margin of 16.2%). We have identified a buying opportunity.

Technical Analysis

We will now estimate the trend of the stock price in the long-run by means of a monthly chart of 10 years and a simple moving average of 12 months:

Figure: McDonald's monthly chart

The overall trend has been generally bullish since mid-2011 but is now stalled in an over-long sideways trend, which is apparently a secondary trend. The price is nearly at maximum level and about to cross the simple moving average of 12 months. Furthermore, the MACD indicates that we are in a bearish period, probably coming to an end because the indicator is very low. The volume has remained stable over the last four years.

Figure: McDonald's weekly chart

Looking at a mid-term chart, in this case a weekly chart of five-years duration, we can observe this sideways trend more clearly. In this case, within this sideways trend, it may be a good time to buy because the fast MACD line has just crossed the slow line and is about to move to positive values. Moreover, adding an exponential moving average of medium speed (20 weeks), we see that it just turned towards a positive trend. Finally, the RSI is in medium values so this information is not relevant.

This sideways movement is confirmed by observing the divergences between the maximum price peaks that are at the same level (there are 3 maximum peaks at around $103) and the maximum MACD or RSI peaks, which are decreasing, although this signal could be interpreted as a premonition of a turnaround.

Should we buy shares, the short-term objective would be the strong resistance at around $103 and we may set a stop-loss at the $94 resistance (since we would be speculating in the short-term). For long-term investments we should be cautious and wait for price to exceed the $103 resistance. As a final strategy combining these two options, we could buy now and put a stop-loss at $94, and when the price exceeds $103 we could move the stop-loss up to this figure and wait for the price to rise even more.

Figure: McDonald's daily chart

Performing the same analysis on a daily chart covering two years, we confirm previous findings regarding the advisability of buying for the short-term. However, in this case, RSI looks overbought, so we might expect a small correction in the coming days.

Security Analysis

The price to be considered for a security analysis is the latest one, or $96 (remember this analysis is being performed in November 2014). However, the last financial report is for the 2013 year-end and so is somewhat outdated. For a company as stable as McDonald's, this is negligible. The most important ratios are:

EPS=5586/990=$5.64 (5.88%)

PER=96/5.64=17.02

Capitalization=96*990Mill=$95.040 Millions

Price/book value=95.04/16=5.94

As a first-look analysis, the EPS is quite good: the company earns $5.64 per year per share, or 5.88% of the share price. The PER seems low and the share price compared to its book value looks reasonable (about 6 times higher).

In any case, we must compare these values to those of other companies within the same sector to ensure that the analysis is valid and relevant. Results are strong in comparison to Burger King, Yum!, and Starbucks. By far, McDonald's outperforms them all:

	BPA	PER	Price/Book
McDonald's	$5.64 (5.9%)	17.02	5.94
Burger King	$0.87 (2.7%)	38.08	8.43
Yum!	$2.36 (3.1%)	21.85	13.20
Starbucks	$2.65 (3.4%)	30.64	12.25

The company participates in the S&P-500 and Dow Jones indices, with a Beta of 0.62 which means a certain level of independence from the indices and low volatility.

Stock market sentiment tells us what most investors/speculators are doing and can be easily deduced from the "Short Percent of Float" (SPF) parameter, which indicates the percentage of shares short-positioned (yes, you can bet that a stock will drop, and I say "bet" because it is pure speculation) for all the free-float. For McDonald's, the SPF is 1.3% (source: Morningstar quotes), which is similar to that of its competitors (Yum! has an SPF of 1.1%, Starbucks's SPF is 1.3%, and Burger King has a big problem with a 40% SPF). In addition, the put/call ratio (the number of bearish options in the market against bullish options, a parameter that indicates what options traders are making) is less than 1%, so options traders are generally bullish on McDonald's.

Finally, on NASDAQ's website (http://www.nasdaq.com/symbol/mcd/insider-trades), we can check what kind of operations the "insiders" are making (insiders are people from inside the company as executives of the top management) over the last year. In the case of McDonald's, these operations are all sales, which is not good news, as it may mean that company executives are dumping their shares.

As for the composition of shareholders, 65.3% of the "float" is in the hands of institutions and 0.04% is controlled by the "insiders."

Conclusion

McDonald's has powerful branding and holds a position of clear market leadership. Its evolution in terms of growth is steady and consistent, and it is present worldwide.

The fundamental data on McDonald's are downright good, with healthy and balanced statements. The level of indebtedness is appropriate and profitability (EBIT) is high. In addition, the company has the capacity to generate positive cash-flows. The DCF valuation is positive, which is to say that there is a buying opportunity because the shares are being undervalued by the stock market. Share price should be around $111, $15 more than the current price.

The security analysis shows an attractive situation compared to other companies, and presents us with an invitation to buy shares. The low volatility and dividends yield make McDonald's a perfect company for long-term portfolios with little risk. However, technical analysis detected no long-term buying signals at the moment, although there are some for the short-term to speculate within a sideways trend.

Keep in mind that the US dollar is strong against the euro right now (EUR/USD = 1.24), which makes shares more expensive to foreign buyers. This factor is very important when buying stocks listed in a different currency.

To summarize, since the parameters that Warren Buffet focuses on to buy stocks are all positive (branding, low debt, high profitability and the ability to generate cash), McDonald's is a great company to invest in for the long-term, and we can say this almost without hesitation. However, it is not clear that this is the best time to buy as a technical analysis reveals no clear opportunity and you may want to wait for the price of the US dollar to drop if your account is in another currency.

DISCLAIMER: This analysis is subjective. It is in no way an attempt to convince the reader to buy or sell McDonald's stocks, but encourages him/her to conduct his/her own research and make his/her own conclusions. It is presented here as an illustrative example of stock analysis.

www.ingramcontent.com/pod-product-compliance
Lightning Source LLC
Chambersburg PA
CBHW070231210526
45168CB00019B/1738